McGinty, Alice B.

Jumping spider

The Library of SPIDERS

The Jumping Spider

Alice B. McGinty

The Rosen Publishing Group's
PowerKids Press™
New York

To Zachary

Published in 2002 by The Rosen Publishing Group, Inc.
29 East 21st Street, New York, NY 10010

First Edition

Book Design: Emily Muschinske
Project Editor: Emily Raabe
Project Consultant: Kathleen Reid Zeiders

Photo Credits: Title page, 14, 17 (top left), 21 (bottom) © David Liebman; p. 5 © Animals Animals; p. 6 (bottom) © Gail Shumway/FPG; p. 6 (top) © Joe Mc Donald/Animals Animals; p. 7 © James Kern; pp. 9, 10 (top) © Microscopix; p. 10 (bottom) © Paul Freed/Animals Animals; p. 11 © Michael Cardwell; p. 13 (bottom left), p. 21(top) © Bill Beatty/ Animals Animals; p. 13 (bottom right), p. 22 © Hans Pfletschinger/Peter Arnold; p. 13 (top) © E.R. Degginer; p. 17 (top right) © Don Brown/Animals Animals; p. 17 (bottom) © Bill Beatty/Animals Animals; p. 18 (top) © G. I. Bernard/Animals Animals; p. 18 (bottom left) © Ed Reschke/Peter Arnold.

McGinty, Alice B.
    The jumping spider / Alice B. McGinty.
        p. cm.— (The library of spiders)
    Includes index.
    Summary: This book introduces "jumping spiders," spiders who leave their webs to search for prey, explaining their physical characteristics, their homes, and their behavior.
    ISBN 0-8239-5568-0
    1. Jumping spiders—Juvenile literature. [1. Jumping spiders. 2. Spiders.] I. Title. II. Series.
    2001
    595.4'4—dc21

Contents

The Jumping Spider

Jumping spiders are some of the world's most colorful and interesting spiders. Of course jumping spiders are great jumpers, too. They can jump up to 40 times the length of their bodies!

Jumping spiders are hunters. Unlike other spiders, they leave their webs to search for **prey**. Jumping spiders can leap onto their victims from high places. The spider uses a dragline to protect itself from falling. A dragline is a silk thread which the spider attaches to a surface before jumping.

This jumping spider is leaping at a fly. You can see the dragline attached to the back of the spider. If the spider is in danger, it can climb back up.

(Top) Jumping spiders have large eyes and furry bodies.

(Left) This jumping spider is eating.

Salticidae

Jumping spiders are in a group, or family, of spiders that scientists call **Salticidae**. There are over 5,000 different **species**, or kinds, of jumping spiders in the Salticidae family. It is the largest family of spiders.

The jumping spider's body is covered with thick hair, often in bright colors and patterns. Male jumping spiders are especially colorful. Many have fringes and tufts of hair on their faces, legs, and bodies. They may also have shiny scales. These colorful decorations often help the males attract female jumping spiders.

There are about 300 species of jumping spiders in the United States. Most species of jumping spiders live in the tropics.

(Right) Unlike most spiders, jumping spiders can see colors.

The Jumping Spider's Body

The jumping spider's body has two main parts. The front part is the **cephalothorax**. Inside it are the spider's brain and stomach. Most spiders' cephalothorax are oval. The jumping spider's cephalothorax is shaped like a rectangle. The rear body part on the jumping spider is the **abdomen**. Inside the abdomen are the spider's heart, lungs, and silk glands. The spider's body is protected by its **exoskeleton**.

Jumping spiders have eight legs. each leg ends in a pad of sticky hair that helps the spider walk on slippery surfaces.

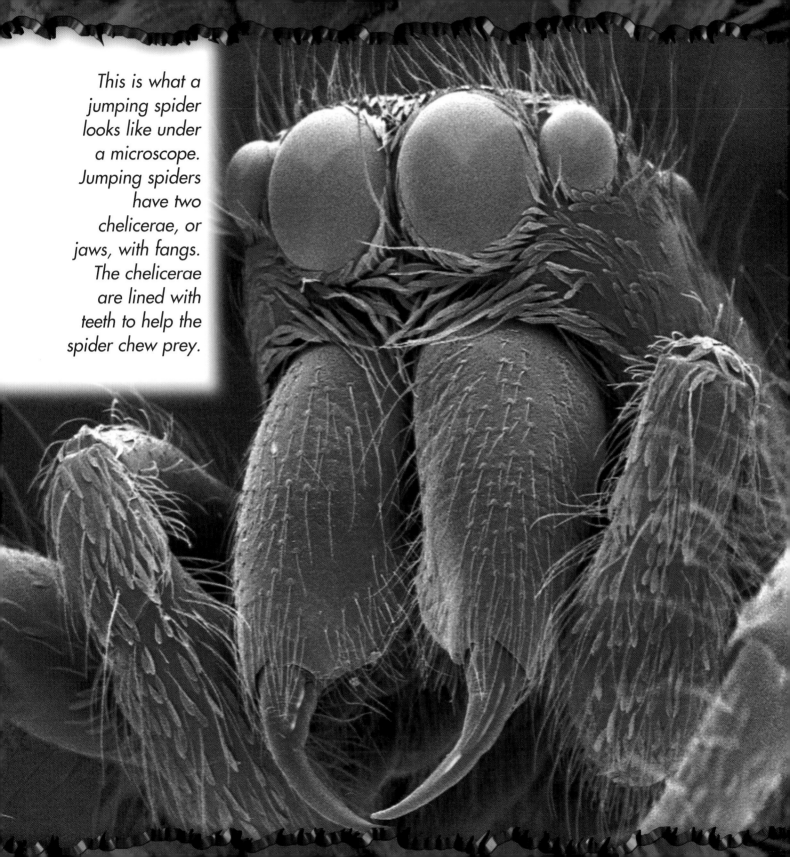

This is what a jumping spider looks like under a microscope. Jumping spiders have two chelicerae, or jaws, with fangs. The chelicerae are lined with teeth to help the spider chew prey.

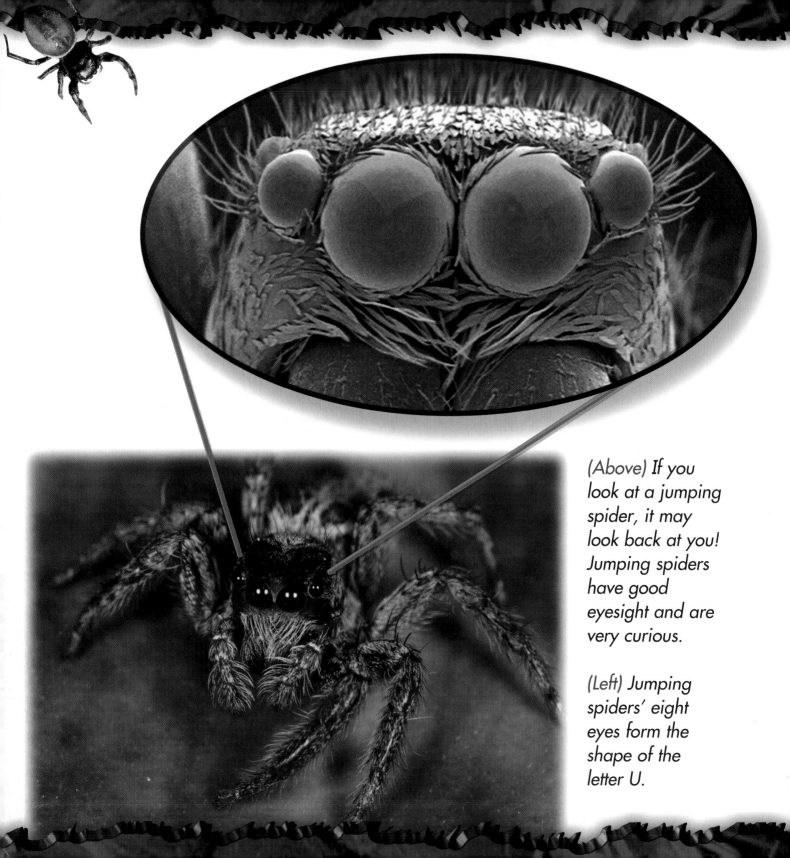

(Above) If you look at a jumping spider, it may look back at you! Jumping spiders have good eyesight and are very curious.

(Left) Jumping spiders' eight eyes form the shape of the letter U.

How a Jumping Spider's Body Works

Jumping spiders have the best vision in the spider world. Their two large eyes can see clear, colorful images up to 12 inches (35 cm) away. The jumping spider's six small eyes can not see clearly, but they can detect motion in many directions. When one of its small eyes detects motion, the jumping spider turns itself around so it can see the object with its two main eyes.

Before the jumping spider jumps, it uses its **muscles** to pull in its legs. Then the spider's heart pumps blood into its legs. The pressure from the blood makes the spider's legs straighten quickly. This makes the jumping spider jump.

(Right) This jumping spider has attacked another spider and is eating it.

11

A Jumping Spider's Home

Most jumping spiders make their homes on plants, in the bark of trees, or under stones on the ground. Some jumping spiders may live in stone walls, or on the outside of buildings. The jumping spider looks for a small crack or crevice in which to build its home. Then, using its **spinnerettes** to spin silk, the spider spins a thick silk bag inside the crevice. The silk bag is the spider's home.

Most jumping spiders stay in their homes at night and on cold days. They can stay warm in their homes, and can hide from **predators**.

(Right) This is a jumping spider on a red leaf.

(Above left) This is a jumping spider on its web.

(Above right) Jumping spiders leave their homes to hunt, unlike other spiders who catch prey in the sticky silk of their webs.

Hunting for Food

Jumping spiders hunt during the day. When the jumping spider spots its prey, it creeps up close, like a stalking cat. The spider leaps onto its prey, and bites it with its fangs. The spider then backs away and waits for the prey to die. The **venom** from the spider's bite **paralyzes** its victim and then kills it. The venom also turns the insides of the prey to liquid. When it is ready, the spider will wander back over and suck the liquid out of the dead prey.

Jumping spiders eat insects and other spiders. They can even leap from high buildings to catch insects in flight. The spider attaches a dragline to the building. After it catches its prey, it will climb back up the dragline.

(Bottom) This jumping spider is sticking a dead beetle to a leaf in order to trick other beetles. The other beetles think that the dead beetle is alive. When they come over to the leaf, the clever jumping spider will have another meal.

(Top right) Jumping spiders stuck many dead beetles to the leaves of this shrub in order to attract prey.

(Top left) This jumping spider is attacking a dragonfly.

Laying Eggs

When a male jumping spider is full grown, he searches for a mate. The male spider shows off his bright colors to the female spider. He may wave his legs or **pedipalps**. He may hop up and down and twirl around like he is dancing. If the female spider is the same species as the male, she may wave her legs or copy the male's dance. If she is not the same species, she may eat him!

During the spring or summer after mating, the female spider lays her eggs. She spins thick silk, lays her eggs on the silk, and rolls them into a sac.

(Top left) This female jumping spider is swollen with eggs.

(Left) If you look in the corner of this web you can see this jumping spider's egg sac.

(Top right) This is a male jumping spider.

(Above) These are baby jumping spiders coming out of their egg sac. They are tiny and pale.

(Left) Within three months a baby jumping spider grows into an adult. It changes color and learns to hunt.

Baby Jumping Spiders

A few weeks after being laid, the spider eggs hatch. Many tiny **spiderlings** chew their way out of the egg sac. The spiderlings climb up high and spin thin silk threads to catch the breeze. The breeze carries the spiderlings away. This is called ballooning. Ballooning is one way for jumping spider babies to spread out to make new homes.

As the baby jumping spiders grow, their hard exoskeletons become too small. They must molt, or shed their old skins. The spider's new skin is soft at first. They must hide inside their homes until their skin hardens. Spiders bend their legs while their skin hardens, to help them stay flexible.

Most jumping spiders live for only a few months. The female spider usually dies shortly after her eggs hatch. Male jumping spiders die soon after mating.

The Jumping Spider's Enemies

Many predators eat jumping spiders, including other spiders and hunting wasps. To protect themselves, some species of jumping spiders pretend to be ants. This helps them hide from predators that do not like to eat ants. Ant-like jumping spiders have long, thin bodies that look like ants. The spiders hold up two of their legs when they walk so they appear to have six legs like an ant. They may wave their pedipalps around in the same way ants wave their **antennae**. These spiders also run around on the ground like ants, instead of jumping.

(Above) Can you tell which "ant" is really a spider in this picture? It is the lowest in the picture.

(Left) The hunting wasp is a deadly enemy of the jumping spider.

Jumping Spiders and People

Most jumping spiders like sunshine. They can be found jumping from stem to stem on plants, or darting around on leaves, tree trunks, or buildings. When jumping spiders see people, they may sit and stare instead of running away. They may even jump onto a person's hand to get food. Some people have trained jumping spiders to jump from finger to finger on their hands. Jumping spiders do not usually bite. If they do bite, their bites are not harmful to people.

Like all spiders, jumping spiders help people by eating harmful insects. Jumping spiders are a special help to rice farmers because they eat the insects that destroy rice crops.

22

Glossary

abdomen (AB-duh-min) A spider's rear body part.

antennae (an-TEN-EYE) Two feelers that are part of an insect's body.

cephalothorax (sef-uh-low-THOR-axhs) A spider's front body part, made up of its head and chest.

exoskeleton (ex-oh-SKEH-lah-ton) The hard outer shell of a spider's body.

family (FAM-ih-lee) A group in which scientists place animals or plants that are similar in some ways.

muscles (MUH-sulz) Tissues that pull on a body part to make it move.

paralyzes (PA-ruh-lyzez)..To make unable to feel or move.

pedipalps (peh-deh-PALPZ) Two short "feelers" attached to the cephalothorax.

predator (PREH-duh-ter) An animal that hunts another animal.

prey (PRAY) An animal that is hunted by another animal.

Salticidae (sal-TISS-ih-dee) The family of spiders to which jumping spiders belong.

species (SPEE-sheez) Groups of animals or plants that are very much alike.

spiderlings (SPY-der-lings) Baby spiders.

spinnerettes (spin-uhr-ETZ) Organs located on the rear of the spider's abdomen that release silk.

tropics (TRAH-piks) The hottest places on earth. The tropics are near the equator.

venom.(VEN-um) A poison passed by one animal into another through a bite or sting.

Index

Web Sites

To find out more about jumping spiders, check out these Web sites:

www.geocities.com/Rainforest/Vines/8983/spiders/spiders.html
http://spiders.arizona.edu/salticidae/salticidae.html
http://spiders.arizona.edu/nasaltshome.html